YOUR BEST AMERICAN MII

*

YOUR BEST AMERICAN MII

✾

LORENZO BARAJAS

NEW MICHIGAN PRESS

TUCSON, ARIZONA

NEW MICHIGAN PRESS

DEPT OF ENGLISH, P. O. BOX 210067

UNIVERSITY OF ARIZONA

TUCSON, AZ 85721-0067

<http://newmichiganpress.com>

Orders and queries to <nmp@thediagram.com>.

ISBN 978-1-934832-99-8. FIRST PRINTING.

Design by Ander Monson.

Cover image by Lorenzo Barajas.

CONTENTS

APPLE EATER

you're so loved by   he who made everything

even your shirt of   ben franklin   and george washington
sharing a blunt   so say

hosanna   pass me around the pews   when in rome,   raw
dog

never sacrilegious   to do anything   so giddy at 6am   it's
practice getting up

for mass   dress rehearsal for   another pieta   habit
forming

distills into a kernel of   amatory feeling   they soak into a
sugar cube   exciting   & tonight

everybody wants a bump of   your spirit in   the abbey

they say whoever gives head to instruction prospers   and
well,

i don't drink all this pineapple juice for nothing   when he said
go   and be *fruitful*   i took it spiritually

like took the earring off my gay ear   and put a more dangly
one on

spare another quarter to light up this reliquary? wanna love
this   damned thing aglow

wipe the lip smudges from your chalice with   holy
thanksgiving   nothing in my palms

but napkin   i say a 't' is just like a cross   great news for
tboys, tgirls everywhere

moses struts in   and says

let those sissies walk

if it feels holy   then maybe it is   cartwheels the aisle

goes back to the ministry   repatriated   to all the non-
collecting departments

your heart   determines your path   & first mine's   right
to your bed   merry i make my pilgrimage   to the

highways   just trying to find some

luv in the apocrypha   in these pages not half as canon as
chicken scratch

breathing clouds through this midnight   lord, so cold on the
nativity's eve   i reach for

a horse blanket   find your hand all over

& know what to call u by touch alone

which to seye in englissh   "hevenes lilie,"   face pretty with the
tells of longing

blessings be on you, angel

for spending so much time on your knees   approche neer and
looke up murily   statue of

rubbed-up bronze underneath

semeth elvyssh in those hips girl   swivel

and at moment of conversion   gentle pasture   not the worst
thing this garden has seen   while waiting to fruit again

in refractory bliss peace   simpage   not the worst   that's
happened   in our lineage

forbid i name the sin of eden   as gluttony   as apple hunger
i think for lent   this year

i'll just give up   period

for this is my body   which is given to you

show me your sundae best   like if it wud indeed please you to
become a stakeholder in my sin   then medium rare?

the usher death drops   a hail mary

jane   divinity dipped in kief, thc, and   maybe chocolate
lindt rollin   we hear: take n breed,   take n breed

& the whole congregation kikis   sunblown by whoever
hijacked   the ave maria karaoke bar fiascopiece   everybody
clutchin robes

setting loose   in another   margaritaville cancun party
cathedral

tbh   at the end of days   all too dim and shiftless to listen to

nunspeak

stupid   beknight me with your bong water girlie

smile like a mouthful of cattle   pregnant   +too fertile not
to be popular at orgies

popet in an arm t' enbrace   or a regular st.teresa

STRIPTEASE OF SPRING

come friday
all those millions of   gay unpaid interns   switch off the
overheads

and pilgrimage   into the tunnels   rocked asleep   elbow to
elbow   through the caffeine crash

into sweaty   ketamine fantasies
an honor to fuck

i keep wanting to ask   how the barista to doc marten
pipeline   is stronger than   my will to live   and other
mysteries

like i work the whole week   and my bank account   can be
tanked by a $30 boysmells candle...

it smells like   it's just me and   all these knickknacks
stuffed into a baggu   i can't

take into heaven

even if i'm good enough   to get there

they get stooped up   rapturously

let's say,   if i blink   and am making corporate graphic art
for a   nonprofit start-up 'collective'

where i have to illustrate   bipoc families   with whippets
in or out of   sweaters

make me rewatch   broad city   bc i was not paying attention

keep me grateful   for every mulberry   that falls into my
hands   so many blessings it

stains the tooth of the wood purple

for gratitudes   that not even mr. kiwi   can sell us

so god,   if you're here tn   on the fire
escape   as my roomie and i   watch the
grackles   puff their throats   the cicadas
the sirens   the smoke draws

this city song   plucked out the window

then yes,   i must believe   to some extent   we are each
other's prayers

heartfemme   every cell wanting to be glittered

beverly glenn copeland   talks about things being   ever new
but instructions unclear

i move to bushwick   the nearest   disco ball bathroom
shared closeness   we all had   the same chronic illnesses
shared pains   medicines   toilets   cranked air filters   us
on the couch   buzzing up capsule orders   or wingstop   &
that toothless bodega cat   drooling with   love for us

here we learn   when the world steals our courage   breaks
our bodies and makes us   hate ourselves

we can go to   the woods   to take polaroids for   our wallets

only *some* of them nudes

how we know   nature is healing

in ny, these places are   close enough to touch

i reach   my first thanksgiving   without my family   but
then again   there was   us   an airbnb cabin   in northern
mass   we wanted to s'mores for dinner   but everything was
closed   so i whipped around our   chevy spark   until we
found marshmallows   at a cvs   which we toast   until they
were black husks   that fell into the   wood stove   glistening
like grackle feathers   a reach away   *the country of anywhere*
/ the roads will take you there

and back again   teaching you how to drive through this
sweet   immortal loop   craggy mountain   of memory

fallen holdings   from the revolutionary times   taste
of   charred beyond sausage   hum of   the toll bridge
husked   just barely

ever new

things we hold   to keep sane   like each other   learning
that we are   everywhere   anytime   ashed history   on
our lunch break   by the hudson   where we throw our
cherry pits   same body that   marsha p johnson   stripped
herself into   praising the god neptune   same docks where
she was dumped in   clocked out forever   in this ocean
miles away from my original   we trade   new bodies to inhabit
ever new

throes of trauma   tease of spring

a reach away   the subway tunnels   the filthiest club
greasy, slingshotting you around a pole

again and again

that lawless underground where
we're slinging elbows   into stuffed up air
with no breeze   going express

as if my spirit could come flying

this knowing that   this train arrived for a body too dirty
for anyone to drink from

late for you, but yes for you

everything in this city for you   everywhere

ashed histories

LARD FANTASY FOR HUSKY BOYS

as the monarchs passed in search of tijuana, beyond the swings
and the running field

they sat on the fence opening and closing like paper

fanning like a palm

into my hands   kissed by a more ancient sun

say this is symmetry and that some things are fragile

do this stretch where i flutter my knees apart

loving what's between

/

at home dad makes us steak   salsa and tortillas made with
lard   all he knows to do   divorced

we eat outside off of plates that look like animals

pick burrs from our socks   chew them out to trade for
peppercorns

no bells anymore, just my stomach rumbling

california is a trick   because it's impossible not to love

every season is the same   sneaking   mirage   straddled
by dry heat   flaming hot red 40   girl boy   technically a
desert tho   and in this place,   stretch marks rake across my
thighs   in angry lines   crisscrossed   i want to say hellfire
all over my body   down chinward   like grill marks   but
itchy

no lock on the door

stained napkins in my   underwear   hoodie around
my waist   which unknots when i run the mile

how much grief   i want to say   explodes

/

hey queen   this is my apology to you

to the back of an empty throat   to the gaps where the light
got in   and twisted up   making you forget

yourself

/

the thing   that aztecs believed,   within us lies
a cave, a gorge   whose only function is to await   that which is
given   whose only function is

to feed

some things aren't so obvious

like girl   yeah,   your razor scooter   is a torture device
for shins   and you keep hopping on it

/

i literally have to squint   not to see   all the   questions
the grease   sparkling on the bag   not to see
whatever on my lip   as quite a mustache

but as a companion for life<3

not to see myself   in the men on mattresses   floating in our
garage

/

i kept flirting with   hope   but he   hated my ass
swung me around like a   plastic nunchuck

/

the jacaranda always lost its flowers   to the yard
crashing   like muscle memory   branches by the end
dried things we plucked   the only skinny thing
by morning   even though i kept   praying   i could be

/

though i knew

hunger is the most american of all feelings   and therefore
could not be trusted

/

bell hooks describes   *the body as an archive of its experiences;*
the body carries with it   *a record of pain*   so i can agree,
a culture that   attributes fatness with excess   *would concur*
that the fat body is an archive   *of suffering*   of   too many
freedoms

/

i bake my blackberries into loaves   scaled out from recipes
made for one   mango mocktails with toasted coconut
dusted on the rim   trays of grilled halloumi   zucchini
pasta   baked mussels   in crushed tomato cans piled with
parm   perhaps a perfect metaphor

for pleasure

/

when my classmate hands me a tiny

paper cup of lemonade

which on the bottom says,

die   in sharpie

instead of crying   i play this computer game   that's just
typing

/

these are the terms of my forgiveness   knocked back

aguacate that speaks of butter   churro-sucked fingers
sweetly   masa, in all its fullness   more dense

ancestors becoming ancestors   like coyotes into lap dogs
just figures   a dance

into an orange los angeles sunset   peel slipped loose
in one go   your love is   my medicine   my sweaty dress
on the floor

/

completely into it   singing out to the queen palm
nothing could be

as done up as you   falling against the   chain link

heavy enough to dent

/

into a holdfast

we reach across the canyon   raked to dirt   thank god   still
here

will the corn be growing a little tonight when I wait in the fields for
you

to say what of the squash   growing squat   to the ground

/

when we finally make it

our home together

it is light filled and beautiful   breeze moves easily from end
to end   it is a pleasure to cook in the sunlight   to laze in it

smell of   great food, spices and curries   pies bread rising
this air   could end you

our spirits   soar into high ceilings

/

smashing against the insides   of my unending cave

MARINE SNOW ECONOMICS

i come bearing anchors   heavy growth   on my jaggedly
indented coast

back in the 1700s,   the dutch were plagued by the shipworm
which nudges the ridges

of its shell   against wood   to burrow is actually a
mollusk   clam-like   dike destroyer

/

all the hulls i could   tunnel into   all that timber i crave
and keep craving

all these ships i down   whistling until   what flesh i have
grows slack

/

and can barely stomach   the sheer joy

when my bf hands me a bowl   with his words circling the lip
it got fucked up

i did not give up   bc i always did

gives me a bottle   of his testosterone   after 6 months
without health insurance

/

care is a message   that says i'll fill your cup when it tilts

/

like if this damaged body still holds me   is mine forever
if the chemistry of the ocean will not be fixed

fibro all along my   spine, joints, and digestive system

if the reef actually bleached itself,
it wasn't professional?

/

plankton blooms   smog makes the sunset smolder   at
least it's gorg out this evening

ru puts her hands on her hips on the rig

and there are more blues than any i've ever seen

miles of netting   hold me

dependable   for things   a handful of people decided
to be a narrative error   and it's no one's fault   or   at least
not ours

/

etymology doesn't lie

if you take the word   shore   to shear,

what a sad ancestry that is   always cutting away   always
somebody's wings clipped   or shore, old norse,   a
temporary support

that's terrifying   all that could just gut out beneath you

and just knowing   the background of   grand theft auto v
has become so advanced   it can run simulations of   sea
levels rising,

can nobody imagine a space where this undoes?

does that not make any more sense   than a feathered, bone
eating worm destroying our

destroyer?

& each year

less and less sand comes back   hazardous structures at
riis beach   exposed   i.e. a wooden groin   bobbing
up shamelessly   spilling whiteclaw   on whatever is   left
because ofc   the end of the world   has gotta be a
gay beach   darty   or at least   mine could be
with you

/

do you like mythical creatures   have u ever pegged a cis

/

we are all chased by   our pasts

the greeks   with all their bounty   would gift their
male lovers   junk,

i.e. dried pollock   anchovy   valentines   bc anything more
would be   full-blown   not just the casual   straight
rubbing bundles of wood together   whispered f

implied   or what i'm saying is
how it felt like   whatever   to lose my virginity   to a man
who asked my ethnicity   mid-thrust

/

and out of a sea of all that   limp driftwood   blank verse for
three years   every crab pot empty   whole ancestries of
countries of tragedy

washed up this perfect   boy of venus   barely gripping the
earth with all his toes   (bc pots)

/

but the blush   the jewel tones of algae   of pixels   stories of
his grandmother   on the coast of jamaica   raising orchids

kisses under his spider plant   as it rained   little white
flowers   onto his locs   little colonizers   on both of our
shores

my eyelids   for a moment   shut

the ocean   brought inside   crashing   brushing against
the hair under his navel   like kelp underwater   anchoring
me to him

/

i promise   there's so much we can learn from each other
i am from birth   a receiver

a consumer like any other which   tells me,

harm is the capacity for industry   and industry meets us

when we're starving

/

the wrack teaches us patience   flexes its tensile strength

tells us that luv   will fill us when we need

carries us in its branches which   *swell into bulbous, almost
heart-shaped structures;   from there these reproductive cells are
liberated*

& isn't that what we all want? just to be full   to be held

what's so scary about a cave,

can you hear your heartbeat   against the walls reverberations
too secret   too shaking

/

a jury of worms writhes in agreement

bro   a couple of gavel hits   would end you

/

the answers   trail in front of us   like the tail of a comet
slightly   overhead of

us creatures sank at   the bottom of the ocean   down
here we know   there's no better way

to end an empire   than with licked fingers

it's a clambake
shells spew their last dew

RIPPLES

i like how the phrase   when i was little   means   when i
was young

because i felt so little when i was young,   and now my dad
and i   have both had the feeling of   the age i have become

hinged at   this point of connection   across a sweet flip of
symmetry

strip to   a sports bra that was once mine,   sun on my back
and   some bug nibbles

gorge myself on enough pita chips to be full   the most
american of all feelings

the most pimple-patched   of all faces   kinda epic   in that
way

how a scar can become the color of gumdrops

it's so easy to miss ny when   you're not there in that #grindset

permastoned with brain fog   cracked phone on an aux
and mismatched socks

god it can be a mouthful

a mouthfeel

and if so, probably frozen yogurt   it's like what if   my
body   had everything it wanted at once   and it was   obsessed
with it

circus animal cookies   bits of   mochi   nutella   green
tea and rambutan   fudged up maximalist realness   yes, it
was cold

toppings   wherever   whenever   some people
didn't like it   because it wasn't ice cream   but for me it was

everything

i just

can't help but suspect   these slays are numbered   when
every record beats the last stat   and gay math is like

i choose not to participate in it

what is my life   but a garbage patch   azealia banks
calls   the 21-zoo

amassing more and more junk to cover with

my favorite genre   of trash   aches, my favorite genre of
pains

ny is not a figurative place   but a real one   that i really want to
say   explodes with items

where the fear of being alone   is a sparkly deep fake of   bbl
level proportions   bc you're literally   splitting

feathers   with the guy next to you   anything or

anyone could be an angel   it's a hard place to be   especially a
pigeon   which i call   a dove in disguise

tells of longing   blessings be on you

something about grackles   ambling on the dirt of   what
little of it   left   making us think we can

survive anything

cinches, cucarachas, ratones
dancing into butterflies

glorious pollution sunset   miles away from my original

an animal crossing town   terraformed to dust *no clouds in
my zones*   only some casualties   no ugly villagers   but we're
like   a dirty little slug   everyone wants to   rid of   with
a squish smear

underfoot

they don't want us to figure out

queers can grow up to be happy queers   who can buy an
almond joy   at any given   moment   not wanting us to
learn   our   sluttiness and   our pop songs   are renewable
resources   and we love each   other   even in this
dump

we learn   not only do we   have to   but the signs are
everywhere   a reach away

the sea wracks have no roots, but instead grip the rocks by
means of   disc-like expansion... congealing,   creating a union
so firm   only the grinding of shore ice can tear it away

is that your tendril grazing me or is it   mine   i've been so
terminally online

i hardly know   if i have the capacity   to read the things
that could save me   let alone write them?

girl we have television now

ripples settle on the hudson   at domino park   a mirage that's
practically cancun to us

but we're addicted to   doing it anyway   committing to
the bit of

miniskirt tennis   melon margarita   papaya salad   sticky
on our vanity pecs   down to our bedazzled canes   there's no
use for   being discreet in the   summer

if cyrée johnson says   femme is a feeling   i say it's a being
you can   bump

in the abbey   i just   really

can't help but suspect these slays are numbered when   every
temp   is a record jumpscare and   every fall falls   faster

and that

makes it more and more important   for me to be telling you
this   if my words dive   headfirst into a pothole   and i keep
saying it   i keep saying it

"are these rosehips?" i ask him over facetime, crouching into
snow, "we could make tea."

"probably, it might be a little dirty. we still have all those juniper
berries." he was right.

"i'll take some," i confer with myself, stuffing a few into thrifted
cashmere. they don't stain and the buds are fragrant

"alright baby. love you."

we have got to   sweep out the magic hiding in the corners and
use it to help each other

you can put almost anything   in a tincture   and take it with
you freely   this healing surrounds us

*long ago   newly born infants   were given downsized versions
of   adult tools, such as items of warfare for   those assigned male*

*(arrows) items of   domesticity for   those   assigned female
(utensils)*

or how some things wound you   before you've had   your first
breath,   they're designed that way   to ensnare   to mark

callosities, a whale lice   appears as patches on a calf   prior
to birth

we inherit these   cycles of pain   which never reached resolve
to oppress   us   into our   deep trenches

but they go no further   if we equip ourselves   to dismantle
them

the wrack curls around us   protecting us, yes liberating us too

would be silly to think   nature isn't on our side   when to be
queer   is to get sweaty

with the   spirit of   biological androgyny   not just sexless
invertebrates

but the copepods   swirling in the tap water   the algae in our
lungs

absorbing 30% of the co2 in the air

the ocean acidifies   becoming harder for   creatures with
shells   to grow them   harder for critters to   protect
themselves   harder to distinguish them from

each other   the city is severed

our history is a sealed   entry point   with no utility   we lift
the manholes to   get a look at   the solace

underneath

emergent gameplay is a term which references a game which
orients you   as you play it

i think   my favorite kinds   are the ones in which randomly
misclicking   works

like bugsnax   or like making a mii   a perfect and beautiful mii

& that shirt   that clings to your stomach   not only showing
its outline   in the fridge glow   but hugging it   and this

will i have   to hold this fridge door open   for long
enough not to want anything inside

i guess   body ecstasy   is a place   i want to live always   but
can only visit   for a little while   like underwater   so i
make a

monument   to that feeling   before my body   glitches

la+tion gl!tch -es. with ☆ the advent of machinery,   elif
answers == 1:   print "it is certain" "concentrate and ask again"
"reply   hazy, try again"

with this   i make a tribute to   the morning songs
filling the conch   the bladder grass   the wrack

all of you   a palm's worth of ash

i like this face,
and i've seen many shores wiped clean

REFERENCED IN THE POEMS

APPLE EATER
walmart merch
bernini, 'the ecstasy of st. teresa'
communion cloth
chaucer, 'the canterbury tales', 'the tale of st. thopas' and 'the
    monk's tale'
lindor truffles
'the song of solomon'

STRIPTEASE OF SPRING
beverly glenn copeland, 'color of anyhow'
cloud print baggu
larry mitchell, 'the faggots & their friends between revolutions'
wingstop lemon pepper rub
m train servive (derragotry)

LARD FANTASY FOR HUSKY BOYS
perfume genius, 'describe'
bell hooks, 'teaching to transgress'
zoopals
ana quiring, 'going with the gut: fatness and erotic knowledge
    in black feminist theories'
pictochat under the covers
arthur russell, 'close my eyes'
cecelia klein, 'snares and entrails: mesoamerican symbols of sin
    and punishment'
manifestation for a new home

MARINE SNOW ECONOMICS
'*i did not give up*', clay vessel by mika cook-wright
kelis, 'shooting stars'
'shore' provided by the online etymology dictionary
black cherry whiteclaw
https://gta-myths.fandom.com/wiki/global_flooding
glover et al, 'bone-eating worms from the antarctic: the
    contrasting fate of whale and wood remains'
anonymous grindr user
rachel carson, 'the edge of the sea'

RIPPLES
elfin forest recreational reserve
azealia banks, '212'
birth rituals in the codex mendoza
tommy pico, 'junk'
hero pimple patches
pest control ad posted at the intersection of myrtle-wyckoff
ocean carbon sequestration
mii, digital avatar
rihanna, 'umbrella', misquote
cyrée johnson, 'slingshot'

LORENZO BARAJAS is an ocean-adoring, queer, trans, and disabled poet of Mexican identity. He has performed his work in barbecues and backyards along the coasts—at a chocolate tasting, under the flower moon, and at a memorial service for Sylvia Rivera. Currently he lives in a double Taurus household in Ridgewood, NY, occupied Munsee-Lenape land, where he continues writing on care ecologies and other such pathways to interconnection.

❁

COLOPHON

Text is set in a digital version of Jenson, designed by Robert Slimbach in 1996, and based on the work of punchcutter, printer, and publisher Nicolas Jenson. The titles here are in Futura, which is the best font for titles.